the generosity habit

HOW DAILY GIVING CAN CHANGE YOUR LIFE
AND TRANSFORM THE WORLD

the generosity *habit*

matthew kelly

BLUE SPARROW
North Palm Beach, Florida

BLUE
sparrow

Copyright © 2021
KAKADU, LLC
PUBLISHED BY BLUE SPARROW

The-Best-Version-of-Yourself and 60 Second Wisdom
are registered trademarks.

ISBN: 978-1-63582-248-9 (hardcover)

Designed by Ashley Dias

10   9   8   7   6   5   4   3   2   1

FIRST EDITION

Printed in the United States of America

"Don't just love, astonish people with your love. Don't just dabble in generosity, live a life of *staggering generosity.*"

table *of* contents

---

PART ONE

17 perspectives *on* generosity

THE GENEROSITY HABIT.

The generosity habit is simple: Give something away every day. It doesn't need to be money or material things. In fact, the philosophy behind the generosity habit rests on this singular truth: You don't need money or material possessions to live a life of staggering generosity.

THE WORLD NEEDS CHANGING.

Everyone knows the world is in need of profound change. We just cannot seem to agree on the best way to go about that. What is most likely to usher in a new era? Politics, education, law, economics, technology, or something else?

It depends largely on what we are trying to accomplish. All these aspects of society should serve human flourishing, but our unbridled quest for more, bigger, faster, and better, seems to have blinded us to how change either ennobles or debases people.

Are you flourishing?

Is your neighbor flourishing?

Is our nation flourishing?

Is the human family flourishing?

The next big leap for humanity will come from rediscovering what it means to be authentically human. It is the very best of our humanity that the world desperately needs now—and generosity brings out the best in people.

THE FUTURE WILL BE PROFOUNDLY HUMAN OR NOT AT ALL.

Last week an Apple II computer manual signed by Steve Jobs sold at auction for $787,487. It was addressed to Julian Brewer, who was 14 years old and writing code for games on his Apple computer when Steve Jobs showed up at his house one day. Julian asked Jobs to sign the manual and it has become one of the rarest autographs in history. But it was the message that Jobs included with his signature that made it truly rare.

Jobs didn't sign autographs. There are very few examples. When people asked for his autograph he would say, "I feel weird doing that," or "Everything at Apple is a group effort," or simply "I don't do autographs."

The message Steve Jobs inscribed on the computer manual reads: "Your generation is the first to grow up with computers. Go change the world!"

That was written in 1980, and over the past 40 years computers certainly have changed our lives and the world.

Now the world needs changing again, but we don't need computers to change the world this time. In fact, the kind of change the world needs now will not be driven by technology of any type.

The future will be profoundly human or not at all. That isn't a dark prediction. It is simply an observation. If we do not learn to ennoble each other there will be no future. It is our humanity that will change the world next: our generosity, our compassion, our love, patience, discipline, gentleness, forgiveness, empathy, and friendship.

We cannot go on debasing ourselves and each other so often and in so many ways, and not expect catastrophic destruction.

It's time to get in touch with the best parts of our humanity—and as the man who gave us the Apple computer, the iPod, and the iPhone wrote all those years ago, "Go out and change the world!"

Generosity is beautifully human. It is at the core of our humanity. It is uniquely human and, at the same time, a reflection of the Divine. Every act of generosity ennobles everyone involved, and each act of generosity changes the course of someone's life and therefore the unfolding of human history.

It's time to embrace the power and nobility of generosity and go out and change the world!

I CAN DO SO LITTLE.

"I can do so little," I hear people say. This may be true. But people ask all the time, "How did the world get to be such a mess?" The answer is so simple and personally convicting that we reject it. The world got to be such a mess because millions of people like you and I didn't do their part.

Your part may be small. I don't know. You don't either. We never really know until we start doing it. Mother Teresa didn't set out to become a global icon and champion of the poorest of the poor. She just set out to do her part.

Do your part. Large or small. Do not let your part become another one of the mindless millions of parts that were abandoned. Decide today, right here, that the world will be a better place because you were here, that you will not let your part go undone. Say it to yourself, out loud, "I will not let my part be left undone."

When they are dying, most people regret not having been more generous. There are some regrets that creep up on us in life, but this is not one of them. Choose to live the rest of your life generously.

GENEROSITY IS CONTAGIOUS.

When you are generous you set off a domino effect. Our generosity may be focused on a particular recipient, but the ripple effect reaches much farther than any of us can see. The good we do lives on in other people, in other places, in other times. Generosity lives on forever.

Generosity is contagious. When one person acts generously, it inspires both the recipients and observers of that generosity to be generous toward others later. Research shows that generosity often spreads by three degrees—from person-to-person to person-to-person. That means that one simple act of generosity can impact dozens or even hundreds of people, most of whom you do not know and will never meet.

GENEROSITY LOOKS GOOD ON YOU.

When I was young, my mother would say things like, "That color looks great on you," or "I really like that shirt on you." I was raised on encouragement, and this is just one example. At every turn, my mother and father encouraged me, and their encouragement was the fuel that launched me into life.

Different things look good on different people, but *some things* look good on everyone—and generosity is at the top of the list. Generosity looks good on you.

So, this week... Call someone just to say hello, tip like you've never tipped before, ask the people you love about their hopes and dreams, give someone an unexpected gift, compliment someone who least expects it, save a life by donating blood, smile generously, give someone a life-changing book, be a generous lover, make someone's day, thank someone for influencing your life, be happy for others when good things happen for them, tell someone you love having them in your life!

You're at your best when you're generous. So, don't just dabble in generosity, live a life of staggering generosity. Astonish people with the boldness of your generosity.

The future of the world depends on generosity. It brings out the best in human beings, it ennobles us in a world where so many things debase us, and generosity is wonderfully contagious. So, get out there and unleash the genius of generosity in your circle of influence.

THE NEXT BEAUTY TREND.

Philosophers and poets have been suggesting that there is a link between moral and physical beauty for thousands of years. It has long been known that generosity increases happiness, confidence, self-esteem, and even physical health. Researchers have proven that giving activates an area of the brain linked with contentment. But a recent study from Indiana University found that people who engage in "giving behaviors" are more attractive physically.

Doing good literally draws our inner beauty to the surface. Let's make being generous the next beauty trend.

REDEFINING GENEROSITY.

One of the biggest obstacles to igniting a generosity movement is the perception that generosity is something financially wealthy people do. Generosity isn't about billionaires giving billions. It isn't elitist. Generosity is for everyone. It is each person—you and me— giving every day, according to our gifts and means.

LIFE TO THE FULLEST.

People who are living life to fullest always have two things in common: they believe the future can be better than the past, and they believe they can do something today to bring about that better future. These are both expressions of hope and empowerment.

Generosity is intrinsically hopeful. It empowers us to participate in the unfolding story of humanity. It reminds us that we can heal the past, soothe the present, and influence the future.

WHAT IS GENEROSITY?

Generosity is the virtue of giving plentifully. It is first and foremost a disposition of the heart. Any act of generosity is an external manifestation of the invisible internal reality. It isn't merely something we do; it is an essential characteristic of who we are. Generosity is a way of life.

GENEROSITY IS CREATIVE.

Generosity is wildly creative. It is always looking for new and interesting, kind, loving, and thoughtful ways to manifest. Listen to the spirit of generosity within you. Allow it to lead you. Generosity is one of the most creative forces within you.

WHO IS IN NEED?

One of the most interesting things about generosity is that I have a much greater need to give than other people need to receive. It may seem counter-intuitive, even ridiculous at first, but it is true.

I need to give much more than they need to receive. The world is full of people whose need to receive is desperate. It is easy to make the mistake of thinking they are most in need. Their need to receive is obvious, but my need to give is hidden. And as desperate as their need to receive appears, my need to give is even more desperate.

We may think we are reaching down to give them a hand up, but perhaps the very opposite is the truth.

The heart of generosity is humility. Focus on your need to give, not their need to receive.

GENEROSITY IS GOOD FOR YOU.

There are so many ways generosity is good for you. Over the past 25 years, there have been hundreds of studies into the effects of giving and generosity, and yet, in many ways they seem to simply affirm what we already knew intuitively or from experience. Here are sixteen ways generosity is good for you:

- Generosity improves your physical health.
- It improves your mood.
- Generous people live longer.
- It evokes gratitude and contentment.
- It enhances our awareness of the meaning and purpose of life.
- Generous people have better relationships.
- It makes us happy.
- It transforms the way we feel about ourselves.
- Generous people tend to have more friends.

- It stimulates a more positive outlook on life.
- It has a mysterious way of rewarding you ten-fold.
- Generosity leads to higher self-esteem, greater life satisfaction, better mental health, lower blood pressure, decreased stress, and the list literally goes on and on.

GENEROSITY FEELS GOOD.

You are not imagining it, and it's not just metaphorical. Generosity literally feels good. Scientists have discovered that one of the reasons is because when you are generous your body releases oxytocin into your bloodstream. This is the hormone that is released during childbirth, sex, breastfeeding, exercise, and while hugging, holding hands, listening to music, and sharing a meal with friends. Oxytocin induces feelings of warmth, euphoria, and connection with others. Generosity produces an oxytocin high.

WE ARE CONFUSED ABOUT NEEDS AND WANTS.

One of the biggest mistakes we make in life is confusing needs and wants. Think about it. What is a need? Formulate a definition in your mind. We often say "I need this," or "I need that," but what definition of need are we operating under?

A need is something that is essential to survive. Needs are necessary to sustain life. Most of what I think I need is not essential for survival. A want is something we desire but can live without. We need so little and want so much.

The world is full of desperate need and destructive want. When we put our wants ahead of other people's needs we abandon our humanity. Which other people? That is the question of questions when it comes to both world affairs and our individual quest to live authentically. All I will say here is that the more we grow in wisdom, the more people we tend to include in our answer to the question.

THE WISDOM OF OPPOSITES.

The opposite of being generous is to be greedy, mean, selfish, stingy, and fearful. You cannot be generous and greedy. Eventually one will extinguish the other. You cannot be generous and mean. You cannot be generous and selfish. Opposites are constantly vying for dominance within you, and eventually one will extinguish the other. Which one? Whichever one you nurture and feed.

EMBRACE YOUR NOBILITY.

People often write to me expressing a desire to live more meaningful lives. It is a yearning that we all experience in different seasons of life. When I write back, this is what I say, "If you want to unleash an endless stream of fulfillment and satisfaction in your life, wake up every morning and try to be more generous today than you were yesterday. A meaningful life is a generous life."

Generosity is a path that will lead you back to the best of your humanity. It is the nobility of your humanity that the world needs at this very moment. We have multiplied and perfected the ways of dehumanizing people. We have woven them into the fabric of society so that many don't even realize they are being dehumanized. We have brainwashed others into believing that they have chosen this dehumanized state.

It is time to unleash a massive re-humanization effort. Generosity is by its very nature rehumanizing, because it announces to the world: "I see you. I hear you. I am with you. I care."

Every act of generosity ennobles another human being. Generosity is a deeply personal and loving response to the needs of other human beings. It announces to the world: "You matter. Your dignity matters. Your nobility as a human being matters."

When we celebrate generosity, we ennoble others and embrace our own nobility. This is the genius of generosity: it brings the best out of us as human beings, ennobles us at a time when so much caters to our lowest self and debases us.

And so it is, we begin to see, that generosity is much more than "random acts of kindness." Anything but random; it is a focused and intentional effort to chart a new course for humanity and the planet we live on.

So, this is my personal challenge to you: Make it a personal ambition to become more generous with every passing day. The mistake we easily make in this area of life is to compare our generosity to the generosity of others. Ernest Hemingway observed, "There is nothing noble in being superior to your fellow man; true nobility is being superior to your former self."

I hope each night when you lay your head on your pillow, you discover that you are more generous today than yesterday, but not as generous as you hope to be tomorrow.

Set out to become the most generous person possible. Astound people with your generosity. Live a life of staggering generosity. Set out to do the most good for the most people. This is life's mandate. And if you listen carefully, you will discover this is what your soul is summoning you to.

PART TWO

101 creative ways
to be generous

generosity is *beautiful.*

#1

Express your appreciation. There are 8 billion people on the planet. 7.9 billion go to bed every night starving to be appreciated.

"True beauty is born through our actions and aspirations and in the kindness we offer to others."

— *Alek Wek* —

generosity is *thoughtful.*

#2

Call someone you haven't spoken to for a while, just to say hello, check in, and see how they are doing.

"No act of kindness, no matter how small, is ever wasted."

— Aesop —

generosity is *creative.*

#3

Catch someone doing something right. So much of our culture is focused on catching people making mistakes. This worldview destroys trust. Children thrive on positive reinforcement, but the truth is we all need positive reinforcement to thrive.

"Let us treat them, therefore, with all the kindness which we would wish to help to develop in them."

— *Maria Montessori* —

generosity is *life-giving.*

4

Plant a tree. Give this gift to the children of today and tomorrow. The air we breathe provides the oxygen we need to live. It also rids the body of waste and toxins. So, breathe deep, plant a tree, and give the gift of fresh air to the people of tomorrow. Being generous with the environment is a way of being generous with future generations.

"If you want happiness for an hour—take a nap.
If you want happiness for a day—go fishing. If you want happiness for a year—inherit a fortune. If you want happiness for a lifetime—help someone else."
— Chinese Proverb —

generosity is *growing.*

#5

Tip generously. Leave a tip that is twice as much as you usually give, or three times.

"Money is like manure; it's not worth a thing unless it's spread around encouraging young things to grow."

— Thornton Wilder —

generosity is *genius*.

#6

Do something to make someone's day. You don't need me to tell you what to do here. The creative genius of generosity is alive and well within you. Seek its counsel and then act accordingly.

"Neither a lofty degree of intelligence nor imagination nor both together go to the making of genius. Love, love, love, that is the soul of genius."

— Wolfgang Amadeus Mozart —

generosity is *teaching.*

#7

Teach. What is it that you know more about than anything else in the world? Whatever it is, don't belittle your expertise, and don't keep it to yourself. Share it with the world. There is someone right now who needs you to teach them what you have spent a lifetime learning.

"Clear is kind. Unclear is unkind."
— *Brené Brown* —

generosity is *supportive.*

#8

Support a small business. Go out of your way to buy something from a small business. Small businesses create 67% of new jobs, deliver 43% of gross domestic product, and produce 16 times more patents per employee than large firms do. 36% of small business are owned by women, 9% by veterans, and 15% by people of color. 68% of every dollar spent with a small business funnels back to the community. Small businesses are literally the backbone of the economy. What you buy, where you buy, and who you buy from can generously reshape your community and the world.

"Our only hope lies in the power of our love and generosity..."

— *Muhammad Ali* —

generosity is *community*.

#9

Bring people together. Host a dinner party, book club, a play date or a picnic in the park. People thrive on connection.

"The way you get meaning into your life is to devote yourself to loving others, devote yourself to your community around you, and devote yourself to creating something that gives you purpose and meaning."

— Mitch Albom —

generosity is *epic.*

#10

Say thank you. Not casually like we do a hundred times every day, but in an epic way. Think about a person who has had an enormous positive impact on your life, seek them out, and thank them like they have never been thanked before.

"Be generous in prosperity, and thankful in adversity.
Be worthy of the trust of thy neighbor,
and look upon him with a bright and friendly face."
— Rainn Wilson —

generosity is *positive*.

#11

Use social media to spread a positive message.

"We all should give what we have decided in our hearts to give, not reluctantly or under compulsion, for God loves a cheerful giver."

— 2 Corinthians 9:7 —

generosity is *unexpected*.

#12

Compliment a stranger. Focus on character rather than appearance. Make eye contact. Expect nothing in return.

"Never worry about numbers. Help one person at a time and always start with the person nearest you."
— Mother Teresa —

generosity is *astonishing.*

#13

Be a generous lover. Don't just love, love generously. Astonish that special person in your life with your love.

"Kindness in words creates confidence.
Kindness in thinking creates profoundness.
Kindness in giving creates love."

— Lao Tzu —

generosity is *exceptional.*

#14

Whenever possible, praise publicly. If we need to provide feedback to a person, it is best to do that privately. But never miss an opportunity to praise publicly. Look for opportunities to praise your children, spouse, friends, coworkers, and people you lead. Public praise can be ten times more effective than private praise.

"Treat a man as he is, and he will remain as he is. Treat a man as he can and should be and he will become as he can and should be."

— Stephen R. Covey —

generosity is *essential.*

#15

Save a life. Give blood. If you have ever been in a situation where you or someone you love has needed blood to survive, you know how vital this gift is to a community. Giving blood is a selfless and noble form of generosity.

"The greatest virtues are those which are most useful to other people."

— *Aristotle* —

generosity is *surprising.*

#16

Give someone an unexpected gift at an unexpected time.

"Kindness is the language which the deaf can hear and the blind can see."

— *Mark Twain* —

generosity is *mindful.*

#17

Be aware of when someone else is in a hurry. Don't concern yourself with the reason, just help them get to where they are going a little faster. Let them in on the highway, allow them to go in front of you in line, help them gather the things they have dropped all over the floor. Simply be helpful getting them to wherever it is they need to get to.

"What wisdom can you find that is greater than kindness?"

— *Jean-Jacques Rousseau* —

#18

Support people who work on the frontlines in any way: the armed forces, first responders, customer service personnel, medical personnel, and moms and dads. Go out of your way to make their lives just a little easier.

"Give what you have. To someone,
it may be better than you dare to think."
— Henry Wadsworth Longfellow —

generosity is *magnanimous.*

#19

Smile. And smile generously. You know what I mean. There is the polite smile and there is a look-them-in-the-eyes-and-make-their-day smile. It's amazing how a generous smile can literally lift people's spirits.

"Too often we underestimate the power of a touch, a smile, a kind word, a listening ear, an honest compliment, or the smallest act of caring, all of which have the potential to turn a life around."

— Leo Buscaglia —

generosity is *selfless.*

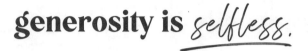

#20

Give someone space when they need it. Most of us are aware when someone needs some time and space to work through whatever it is they are working through. It is loving and generous to give them that space. Don't hover. Don't ask them every five minutes if they are okay. Just give them the space they need.

*"Three things in human life are important.
The first is to be kind. The second is to be kind.
And the third is to be kind."*

— Henry James —

generosity is *visionary*.

#21

Ask someone what their dreams are and help them accomplish one of their dreams. We all need people to help us fulfill the dreams that have been placed in our hearts.

"A tree is known by its fruit; a man by his deeds. A good deed is never lost; he who sows courtesy reaps friendship, and he who plants kindness gathers love."

— Basil the Great —

generosity is *lavish.*

#22

Be generous with your time. When you are with people, pay attention to their desire to continue the conversation or draw the conversation to an end. People often have one more thing they would like to discuss, but they are hesitant to raise it. It is sometimes the most important matter. Choose a situation, meeting, or conversation today and be lavish with your time.

""Let us develop a kind of dangerous unselfishness."
— Martin Luther King, Jr. —

generosity is *encouraging*.

#23

Encourage someone. We all need a little encouragement from time to time. Keep your eyes wide open for the people who cross your path who need encouragement.

"As human beings, our job in life is to help people realize how rare and valuable each one of us really is, that each of us has something that no one else has—or ever will have—something inside that is unique to all time. It's our job to encourage each other to discover that uniqueness and to provide ways of developing its expression."

— *Fred Rogers* —

generosity is *dedication.*

#24

Work hard. Working hard is a way of being generous to your coworkers and customers. It also builds character and soul strength.

"Charity can be a lifestyle, not merely an occasional gift. Read charitably. Give the author your most rational interpretation. Listen charitably. Donate your undivided attention. Work charitably. Be generous with your expertise. In this way, you make charity a daily habit."

— James Clear —

generosity is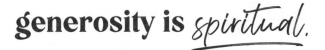

#25

Pray. Pray for someone like you have never prayed for anyone ever before.

"You will be enriched in every way for great generosity..."
— *2 Corinthians 9:11* —

generosity is *personal*.

#26

Get involved. Become a volunteer. Pick something that you are passionate about and allocate a specific amount of time to volunteering each day, week, month, year. Whatever your place or space in life, work out how you can best serve others. It may be for one hour a week, or it may be for one weekend a year. And if you see a need, volunteer before you are asked. Generosity is proactive.

"When you become detached mentally from yourself and concentrate on helping other people with their difficulties, you will be able to cope with your own more effectively. Somehow, the act of self-giving is a personal power-releasing factor."

— *Norman Vincent Peale* —

generosity is *patient.*

#27

Listen. Set aside your thoughts, ideas, and agenda, and really listen to what the other person is saying to you. Listening is the most important communication skill. More than 45% of our time communicating is spent listening. 9% writing. 16% percent reading. 30% percent speaking. Most people wish the people close to them were better listeners. Become a generous listener.

"Mutual caring relationships require kindness and patience, tolerance, optimism, joy in the other's achievements, confidence in oneself, and the ability to give without undue thought of gain."

— *Fred Rogers* —

generosity is *elevating*.

#28

Support a struggling artist. Buy an album from an unknown musician, buy a first-time author's book, hang at least one piece of original art in your home. Artists of all types play a critical role in our individual lives and in the life of society as a whole. When artists follow the call that has been placed upon their lives, they embolden our hearts, enlighten our minds, and elevate our souls.

"Creative people depend on the generosity and graces of strangers."
— Wayne Gerard Trotman —

generosity is *counter-cultural.*

#29

Refrain from judging people. Give people the benefit of the doubt. Assume that they had the best intentions.

"It's not our job to play judge and jury, to determine who is worthy of our kindness and who is not. We just need to be kind, unconditionally and without ulterior motive, even—or rather, especially—when we'd prefer not to be."

— *Josh Radnor* —

generosity is *lighthearted.*

#30

Make someone laugh. Say something funny, foster a lighthearted environment, email someone a joke or a link to your favorite comedian. Humor plays a vital role in human flourishing. It is good for the heart, mind, body, and soul.

"A little nonsense now and then is cherished by the wisest men."

— *Roald Dahl* —

generosity is *proactive*.

#31

Be proactive. Offer to get someone more water or wine when you notice their glass is almost empty. Do something you know needs doing before you are even asked. Preempt problems and prepare solutions.

"In a world of bluff and smoke, real action and true helpfulness are perhaps the ultimate charm."

— Robert Greene —

generosity is *brilliant.*

#32

Send flowers. Send an amazing woman you know flowers. Send an amazing man you know a plant for his office (most men's offices could use one). Plants and flowers remind us that life is beautiful but fleeting, and that seasons come and go.

"Of the various kinds of intelligence, generosity is the first."

— John Surowiecki —

generosity is *persistent.*

#33

Give a monthly gift to a charity that is having an impact in the world. Start with just $10 a month, and challenge yourself to increase it every year for the rest of your life.

"Not being able to do everything is no excuse for not doing everything you can."

— Ashleigh Brilliant —

generosity is *resourceful.*

#34

Declutter. All those things you have that you never use or seldom use? Someone needs them. Be generous with yourself by decluttering your life, and be generous with others by passing these things along to someone else who needs them.

"One man's trash is another man's treasure."
— Hector Urquhart —

generosity is *compassionate.*

#35

Visit the lonely. It's amazing how many lonely people there are on this planet. The elderly are among the worst-affected by this disease. Set some time aside to visit an elderly person in your neighborhood or stop by a local nursing home. Ask questions about their lives, and then just sit and listen. Ask them what was happening in their lives when they were your age. Ask them what advice they would have for young people today. Our culture desperately needs the wisdom and perspective of those who have lived a long time.

"How far you go in life depends on your being tender with the young, compassionate with the aged, sympathetic with the striving and tolerant of the weak and strong. Because someday in your life you will have been all of these."

— *George Washington Carver* —

generosity is *tender.*

#36

Pick up trash. If you visit one hundred cities around the world, it's amazing what you discover just by observing how much trash is on the streets. Make your street, town, and city a place people can feel proud to call home. We can do this is dozens of ways, and one of the simplest is by picking up trash. The way we approach little things impacts the way we approach all things. The earth is an amazing place. Let's try not to forget that it is on loan to us from future generations.

"No one is useless in this world who lightens the burdens of another."
— Charles Dickens —

generosity is *for everyone.*

#37

Save. Generosity is for everyone, including you. It's important to be generous with others, but it is also important to be generous with ourselves. And being generous with ourselves usually ends up benefitting everyone else in our lives and even people we will never know. One of the ways we can be generous with ourselves is by being financially responsible. Saving a little of all you earn is a way to provide generously for your future and those who depend on you.

"Generosity wins favor for everyone, especially when it is accompanied by modesty. "
— *Johann Wolfgang von Goethe* —

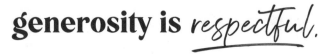

#38

Be on time. Are you a thief? Most people are not and most of us would never even consider stealing. But being late is a form of theft. And it's one of the most offensive forms of theft, because you are stealing something that cannot be replaced: a person's time. Being on time, preferably a few minutes early, is a beautiful way to respect and ennoble people, and a simple way to be generous every day.

"We don't need to share the same opinions as others, but we need to be respectful."

— Taylor Swift —

generosity is *timeless.*

#39

Remember. Remember people's names, remember other people's birthdays and anniversaries, and help those you love to remember their story and your story together. Memories have a powerful positive impact on us psychologically. Go through your photos and send one to someone reminding them about a great memory. Ask people to tell you about some of the best moments of their lives. When we forget our story, we go mad. This is true for a person, a couple, a family, a business or organization, and a nation. Help people to remember their stories.

"Perhaps the best conversationalist in the world is the man who helps others to talk."

— John Steinbeck —

generosity is *innovative.*

#40

Give someone one of your vacation days. Vacation days are more precious at different times in our lives than others, depending on what is happening in our lives or the season of life we are in. Look around the organization you work with and ask yourself, "Who could most use an extra vacation day this year?"

"Never hesitate when you have an impulse toward charity."

— Mark Manson —

generosity is *life-saving.*

#41

Learn CPR. Being prepared to help when the unexpected happens is an incredibly thoughtful way to be generous. Only 54% of Americans know CPR and the American Heart Association estimates that up to 200,000 lives could be saved each year if CPR was performed early enough.

"You cannot do a kindness too soon,
because you never know how soon it will be too late."
— *Ralph Waldo Emerson* —

generosity is *hopeful.*

#42

Be an ambassador of hope. There is enough gloom and doom in this world. Let your presence and words be filled with hope and encouragement. We all need hope. Sometimes we are aware of this truth, and at other times we are oblivious. But when life strikes a blow and our hope fades, we become intimately aware of how important hope is to our well-being. Someone close to you needs a little hope today. Find that person and be an ambassador of hope. Take an interest. Love and care increase hope. Be with a person. Knowing that we are not alone increases hope. Remind that person that while there are ups and downs, life is a wonderful gift. Offer to help. Everyone is carrying a heavy burden. Most people don't expect you to make their life easy, but everyone wishes life could be just a bit easier on days when they are long on troubles and short on hope.

generosity is  practical.

#43

Keep an extra umbrella in your car so you can give it to someone who gets stuck in the rain.

"Love is an exchange of gifts,' Saint Ignatius had said. It was in these simple, practical, down-to-earth ways that people could show their love for each other. If the love was not there in the beginning, but only the need, such gifts made love grow."

— Dorothy Day —

generosity is *vivacious.*

#44

Nominate someone for an award. Very often the people who most deserve awards don't receive them because the people who know of their goodness and genius don't nominate them.

"Love is giving a piece of your soul to another. Life is seeing that celestial fire kindles an eternal flame of joy."

— Anonymous —

generosity is magical.

#45

Give someone their best Christmas ever. Food and gifts, a tree and decorations. Christmas is magical, but not everyone gets to experience the magic. You may not be able to change that for everyone, but you can probably change it for one person or family.

"Kindness is like snow. It beautifies everything it covers."
— Kahlil Gibran —

generosity is *kind.*

#46

Donate your hair. Men, women, and children of all ages suffering from diseases that are ravaging their bodies need hair for wigs. Consider growing your hair out to donate it. You typically need between eight and fourteen inches. This will require real effort, it will be inconvenient, and you will likely suffer many bad hair days both before and after you donate your hair. But imagine losing all your hair and imagine how much of a difference your hair will make in another person's life.

"You can be rich in spirit, kindness, love and all those things that you can't put a dollar sign on."
— Dolly Parton —

generosity is *humble.*

#47

Give intentionally. We give intentionally by weighing how our giving can have the most impact, but there are dozens of aspects to intentional giving. Generosity is not boastful, but it isn't always anonymous. Sometimes it is helpful to make your giving public, because your generosity will inspire other people to be generous. It is possible for the whole world to know about your good deeds and remain humble. When you are giving, make a conscious decision for your gift to be acknowledged publicly or remain anonymous based on which approach will do the most good in each situation.

"Generosity starts when ego ends."
— Maxime Lagacé —

generosity is *comprehensive*.

#48

Buy a journal and write down 100 things you love about someone. One per page. And then give it to them as a gift. It could be a spouse, a friend, a child, a parent. We never articulate many of the things we love about each other. Generously speak your love.

"It's not how much we give,
but how much love we put into giving."
— Mother Teresa —

generosity is *caring.*

#49

Give someone a foot massage. Human touch is critical to human flourishing. Babies can actually die from lack of human touch. When you know someone is exhausted at the end of a long day, offer to give them a foot massage. Massaging the feet provides many physical and emotional benefits, but it is especially powerful at relieving stress and anxiety.

"Sometimes it takes only one act of kindness and caring to change a person's life."
— Jackie Chan —

generosity is *courageous.*

#50

Stand up for someone who is being treated unjustly. Injustice is all around us and takes many forms. It thrives when men and women of goodwill notice it but choose not to get involved because it is inconvenient. There is a lot of talk about bullying in school, but it seems in almost every environment people are bullied today. It's a horrible thing to see the way bullying can affect a child, now and for the rest of their life. It is no less degrading and dehumanizing to see an adult bullied.

"Bad men need nothing more to accomplish their ends, than that good men should look on and do nothing."
— *John Stuart Mill* —

generosity is *big-hearted.*

#51

Forgive. We have all been hurt by others, we have all been betrayed in ways large or small, we have all been the victims of wrongful acts or injustice. Everybody needs to forgive somebody. Forgiveness is a supreme form of generosity. Set out along the road of forgiving someone who has wronged you. And begin to explore how you need to forgive yourself too. Sometimes it is our inability to forgive ourselves for something completely unrelated that holds us back from forgiving other people.

"Two works of mercy set a person free: Forgive and you will be forgiven, and give and you will receive."

— *Saint Augustine* —

generosity is *ingenious.*

#52

Buy the most expensive item on a gift registry. These are often the items a person or couple needs the most, they are also often the items that do not get purchased. You may be thinking, "I could never afford to do that." Not so. Remember, generosity is creative. Split it with a friend or gather a group to go in on it together. Just don't let what you can't do get in the way of what your heart is calling you to do.

"You will discover that you have two hands. One is for helping yourself and the other is for helping others."

— Audrey Hepburn —

generosity is *liberating.*

#53

Try to take the best photo that has ever been taken of someone. We live in an age where almost everyone has a camera that is 100 times better than the best camera available when our grandparents were born. We take lots of photos. But few people or couples have a photo of themselves that they really like. Let's change that.

"I have found that among its other benefits, giving liberates the soul of the giver."

— *Maya Angelou* —

generosity is *optimistic*.

#54

Write a letter. We get hundreds of messages in a variety of forms, but when was the last time you got a real letter, handwritten and from the heart? Letter writing is an art form. Love letters, protest letters, letters of invitation and resignation, letters that started wars and ended wars, letters that comforted and consoled, and letters that kept recipients up at night. Letters between friends, from parents to children, and vice versa. Historians have studied whole lives just through the letters a person wrote. Let's not lose the deeply personal art form of letter writing. Sit down today and write someone a letter.

"You give but little when you give of your possessions.
It is when you give of yourself that you truly give."
— Kahlil Gibran —

generosity is *helpful.*

#55

Surprise someone. Rake their leaves, help with a flat tire, shovel snow, or mow the lawn. Do some good and practical thing for someone else. More than the act itself, it will remind people that in this world that can often seem uncaring and dark, there are still plenty of people who are caring and living in the light.

"It is better to light one candle than to curse the darkness."
— Confucius —

generosity is *comforting.*

#56

Leave someone an unforgettable voicemail. Have you ever received a voicemail from someone special or a message that was so special you never deleted it? A few weeks ago, I met with a woman whose husband died about a year ago. He was a very good friend of mine. "Somedays I have trouble remembering his voice," she said to me. I took out my phone and played her a voicemail from three years ago that her husband had left me. We sat there and cried together as we listened to it over and over again.

"Generosity takes an open heart and a love that asks for nothing in return."

— *Anonymous* —

generosity is *aware.*

#57

Pay attention. Look at the people you encounter today. Really look at them. See them. Most people feel unseen. Listen to the people you encounter today. Really listen to them. Hear them. Most people feel unheard. Go above and beyond to understand the people you encounter today. Seek to understand their perspective and what it is they are going through. Understand their plight. Most people feel misunderstood. Pay attention to the people in your life. Notice when their energy or mood is a little off, and ask if there is anything you can do to make their day a little smoother or sweeter.

"Attention is the rarest and purest form of generosity."
— *Simone Weil* —

generosity is *honest.*

#58

Tell the truth when someone asks for guidance or advice. Not in a way that is hurtful or harmful, but in a way that gently encourages them to look at situations and themselves as they really are.

"The greatest gift you ever give is your honest self."
— Fred Rogers —

generosity is *everywhere.*

#59

Share good news. Every time you hear about something wonderful that has happened, tell five people about it. Email your local news and tell them about good things that are happening in your city or community.

"In the end, maybe it's wiser to surrender before the miraculous scope of human generosity and to just keep saying thank you, forever and sincerely, for as long as we have voices."

— Elizabeth Gilbert —

generosity is *entrepreneurial.*

#60

Help someone who is starting a new business. Buy something from the business, share a key contact who might become a customer or valued vendor, and spread the word about the business. 20% of new businesses fail within the first year. 45% fail within the first five years. We need entrepreneurs to take risks. New businesses stimulate the economy, create jobs, and contribute to vibrant communities. Very often when someone starts a new business, they are risking everything they have. Reward that courage with your generous support.

"Live simply and appreciate what you have.
Give more. Expect less."

— Stephen R. Covey —

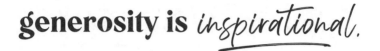
generosity is *inspirational.*

#61

Text a different inspirational quote to the same person each day for a week.

"Don't judge each day by the harvest you reap, but by the seeds you plant."

— Robert Louis Stevenson —

generosity is *grateful.*

#62

Go out of your way to thank the people who serve you in public settings. The staff who clean your hotel room, the custodians who clean public bathrooms, the wait staff at dining functions, men and women who serve in the armed forces, first responders, and those that hold public office. Gratitude is a beautiful expression of generosity.

"When we give cheerfully and accept gratefully, everyone is blessed."

— *Maya Angelou* —

generosity is *togetherness.*

#63

Gather a small group of friends and cook them a meal. Preparing and sharing food has always been at the center of all civilizations and all human relationships. Sharing food builds trust, strengthens connection, facilitates conversation, fosters mutual respect, and leads us to understand each other in new and deeper ways.

"We cannot live only for ourselves. A thousand fibers connect us with our fellow men."
— *Herman Melville* —

generosity is *friendly.*

#64

Pay for the next person in line.

"God comes right out and tells us why he gives us more money than we need. It's not so we can find more ways to spend it. It's not so we can indulge ourselves and spoil our children. It's not so we can insulate ourselves from needing God's provision. It's so we can give and give generously."

— Randy Alcorn —

generosity is *generative.*

#65

Call your mom. Call your dad. Parents are a practical and mysterious part of God's plan for our lives. Sometimes we take them for granted, sometimes we are overly critical, and sometimes we overanalyze those relationships. Living or dead, present or absent, take some time just to be with your parents.

"Charity begins at home but should not end there."
— Francis Bacon —

generosity is 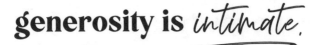 intimate.

66

Ask someone how they are doing. Not in passing. But sit down, take your time, and really listen.

"Listen with regard when others talk. Give your time and energy to others; let others have their own way; do things for reasons other than furthering your own needs."

— *Larry Scherwitz* —

generosity is *all-encompassing.*

#67

Hug generously. The thing about generosity is that it can be applied to almost everything. Our generosity or lack of generosity is apparent in almost everything we do. We have all given and received generous hugs and stingy hugs. Give someone a generous hug today.

"Your own soul is nourished when you are kind; it is destroyed when you are cruel."

— King Solomon —

generosity is *merciful.*

#68

Feed the hungry. Millions of children go to bed hungry each night in our own country, and hundreds of millions around the world. People may disagree on many things, but surely, we can all agree that no child should go to bed hungry.

"Our greatest social responsibility is to demonstrate to all others how to live in this world of hunger, sorrow, and injustice with generosity, dignity, and decency."

— *Chris Ernest Nelson* —

generosity is *benevolent.*

#69

Write an amazing review for your favorite song, book, or product. These are someone's life's work. If they have enriched your life, share that with the world.

"Not for ourselves alone are we born."
— *Marcus Tullius Cicero* —

generosity is *heroic.*

#70

Do something heroic. Don't just be kind, be heroically kind. Don't just be patient, be heroically patient. Don't just be helpful, go above and beyond the extra mile and be heroically helpful. We are all capable of rising above mediocrity and accomplishing excellence. We are all capable of rising above excellence and being heroic.

"Tenderness and kindness are not signs of weakness and despair, but manifestations of strength and resolution."
— Kahlil Gibran —

generosity is *dignified.*

#71

If you cannot say something nice, don't say anything at all. Holding your tongue, keeping your thoughts to yourself, avoiding gossip, sometimes these are the kindest, gentlest, most respectful ways to honor another person's dignity.

"Be generous with kindly words, especially about those who are absent."

— *Johann Wolfgang von Goethe* —

generosity is *enduring.*

#72

Create a legacy. Decide what you would like your legacy to be, how you would like the world to be different because you were here, and work toward it tirelessly.

"A generous person will prosper."
— *Proverbs 11:25* —

generosity is *intentional.*

#73

Pick a book that changed your life and give ten people a copy of that book. Invite each person to let you know when they have read it, so you can go to coffee and talk about the book. Most won't take you up on meeting for coffee, but some will, and those conversations will be soul-altering. Don't forget Jesus healed ten lepers, and only one came back.

"Without love, deeds, even the most brilliant, count as nothing."

— *St. Therese of Lisieux* —

generosity is daring.

#74

Be generous with yourself. Go somewhere you have always wanted to go. Do something you have always wanted to do. Buy something you have always wanted to buy. Give yourself some time. We talk about generously sharing our time with others, but sometimes we are stingy with ourselves.

"The measure of your success will be the measure of your generosity."

— *Pope John Paul II* —

generosity is *humanizing.*

#75

Ask a homeless person her name. Ask a homeless person how he ended up living on the streets. Our names and our stories are important, theirs are too. Give them some money or offer to buy them some food. Many stores won't let them come in even to buy something. Give to them in a way that ennobles them, and reminds them that in a world that may seem indifferent to them there are still some who care. And remember, when it comes to a homeless person, the important word is person.

"Generosity is the flower of justice."
— Nathaniel Hawthorne —

generosity is *amazing.*

#76

Who do you know who needs a break? Everyone needs a break from time to time, but when we are amid life's daily pressures, we may not recognize that. Those around us will likely see it before we do. If you see that someone needs a break, and you can give them a break for fifteen minutes, or an hour, or an afternoon, do that. It's amazing how even fifteen minutes to catch our breath and collect our thoughts can make all the difference.

"The more generous we are, the more joyous we become."
— William Arthur Ward —

generosity is *enchanting.*

#77

Next time you are at a gathering, focus your emotional intelligence on identifying the person in the room who is hurting the most, or the person who least wants to be there. Go out of your way to spend time with that person and lift his or her spirits.

"This brief lifetime is my opportunity to receive love, deepen love, grow in love, and give love."

— Henri Nouwen —

generosity is *inviting.*

#78

Invite someone. There is something wonderful about being invited. It is life-giving to be included. Extend an invitation to someone.

"I want to be a noticer of the good and eager to speak the rare word... a kind word."

— Lysa Terkeurst —

generosity is *altruistic.*

#79

Be selfless. Ask yourself: What is the selfish thing to do here? What is the selfless thing to do here? Choose selflessness. Self-interest is not the purpose of life, and we are not inevitably trapped in a world of suffering and adversity. We can choose to make the world a kinder, gentler, fairer world with our generosity.

"Every man must decide whether he will walk in the light of creative altruism or in the darkness of destructive selfishness."

— Martin Luther King, Jr. —

generosity is *ethical*.

#80

Examine you values. Are your values generous?
How can your values be more generous?

"A man is not to be measured by the virtue of his described actions or the wisdom of his expressed thoughts merely, but by that free character he is, and is felt to be, under all circumstances."

— Henry David Thoreau —

generosity is *expansive.*

#81

Calculate what percentage of your income you gave to charity last year. Give 1% more this year. Give 1% more each year until it simply is no longer possible to give more and fulfill your responsibilities. You will be amazed how this one habit will change your life in one hundred ways.

"A single act of kindness throws out roots in all directions, and the roots spring up and make new trees."

— Amelia Earhart —

generosity is *curious.*

#82

Be curious about people. Everyone you will ever meet has a story. Be curious about their journey. What is it that brought them to where they are today? Like you, there is something they know more about than anything else in the world. Be curious about what that topic is.

"You can make more friends in two months by becoming interested in other people than you can in two years by trying to get other people interested in you."

— *Dale Carnegie* —

generosity is *astounding.*

#83

Mentor someone. A mentor is an experienced and trusted advisor. Who could benefit most from your mentorship? Offer to mentor someone for one year. Meet with that person once a month with no agenda other than to be helpful so they can grow, succeed, flourish, and thrive. Being a mentor is one of the most astounding gifts you can give a person.

"The meaning of life is to find your gift. The purpose of life is to give it away."

— Pablo Picasso —

generosity is *responsive.*

#84

Respond to the needs of others. When a need arises in one person, an impulse arises in another person to respond to that need. Pay attention to those impulses.

"Unless someone like you cares a whole awful lot, nothing is going to get better. It's not."

— Dr. Suess —

generosity is *paradoxical.*

#85

Pay your taxes with a spirit of generosity. The way we approach something can completely change our experience of that thing. Taxes are a perfect example. See your taxes as your generous contribution to society, to helping build schools, roads, and hospitals, rather than as something that is being taken from you. You have to pay them either way. Some might say, you have no choice. But that's not true. You get to choose your attitude. The attitude you hold in your heart and mind determine everything in these situations.

"Life is a boomerang. What you give, you get."
— *Anonymous* —

generosity is *virtuous.*

#86

Contain your frustration. When somebody does something that really frustrates you, something that absolutely drives you crazy, take a deep breath and allow the moment to pass.

"To practice five things under all circumstances constitutes perfect virtue; these five are gravity, generosity of soul, sincerity, earnestness, and kindness."

— Confucius —

generosity is *gracious.*

#87

Receive graciously. There is a generous way to receive a gift. Learning to gratefully and graciously receive other people's generosity is itself a form of generosity. Next time you are the beneficiary of someone else's generosity, be mindful of how graciously you respond.

"We should give as we would receive, cheerfully, quickly, and without hesitation; for there is no grace in a benefit that sticks to the fingers."

— Seneca —

generosity is *romantic*.

#88

Do something romantic. Romance stirs the soul in its own unique way. Be a little more affectionate, thoughtful, helpful, present, and consistent. Light a single candle for dinner. Speak your love. Leave a note hidden somewhere you know it will be found during the day. Slow dance for no reason at all. Plan a getaway. Talk about your fondest memory of each other. Be generously romantic.

"You can give without loving,
but you can never love without giving."
— Robert Louis Stevenson —

generosity is _healthy._

#89

Hydrate. Give yourself the gift of hydration. Drink 64 ounces of water each day for a week and take note of the changes you notice. Hydration affects many health factors, but it also impacts our ability to concentrate and our mood. It's hard to be aware when you cannot concentrate, and awareness is essential to live a generous life. And it's hard to be generous when you are in a bad mood. Generously hydrate yourself so you can be mindful of other people's needs and generously meet them.

"You do not have to be rich to be generous."
— Anonymous —

generosity is *uplifting.*

#90

Tell someone what you admire most about them.

> *"Those who are happiest are those who do the most for others."*
>
> — Booker T. Washington —

generosity is *beyond.*

#91

Buy someone your favorite thing. When we give our possessions away, we usually give the things we don't need or want. Do something different this time. Go beyond the low bar our society sets for generosity. Think about something you own that you just love. You know it's just a material possession, but nonetheless it brings you great joy. I'm not asking you to give it away, I'm challenging you to buy another one for someone else. If you have to save to accomplish this generous feat, come up with a plan to save what is needed. And most importantly, think, pray, reflect, discern, who is likely to derive as much joy from it as you do. That is the person to whom you should give this fabulous and insanely thoughtful gift.

generosity is *purposeful.*

#92

Ask for help. Sometimes the most generous way to engage another person is to ask them for help. There are many people in this world who believe their lives have no meaning and purpose. And nothing makes us feel a greater sense of purpose than genuinely helping someone else.

"True kindness is not necessarily giving something to someone who is down, but showing them that they still have something to give to get back up."

— Charles F. Glassman —

generosity is *problem-solving.*

#93

Conserve water. Two of the most significant crises humanity will face over the next 100 years will surround clean air and fresh water. More than two billion people do not have access to clean and safe drinking water today. This has been largely considered a third-world problem, but in our lifetimes water shortages will become a first-world problem. Bottled water is already more expensive than Coca-Cola. Imagine a world where water is more expensive than gas for your car. Impossible? Maybe. Maybe not. Regardless, we are stewards of water like all of God's gifts, and therefore have a responsibility to use water wisely. There are two aspects to water conservation: using water intentionally and preventing wasteful usage.

generosity is *sacrificial.*

#94

Give until it hurts. Just try it once. Give in a way that requires you to change your lifestyle in some way large or small.

"Live simply so others may simply live."
— Mahatma Gandhi —

generosity is *gentle.*

#95

Create some whitespace on your calendar. Clear your schedule for a day or a week. Spend some time reflecting on life: where you are, were you've been, and where you would like to go. Decide to do less and be more. Be gentle with yourself. If we can learn to be gentle with ourselves when that is what is called for, we will have the wisdom to be gentle with others.

"Generosity is giving more than you can, and pride is taking less than you need."

— Steve Maraboli —

generosity is *understanding.*

#96

When someone argues with you or is rude toward you, look beyond what they are doing and saying. There you will find their hurt. You will most likely discover that what they are doing or saying has nothing to do with you. It is a reaction to the hurt they are feeling. What people do and say is interesting. Why people do what they do and say what they say is fascinating. Always look beyond people's words and actions for their reasons and motives. Compassion is born from trying to stand in another person's place and experience what they are experiencing.

"Kindness begins with the understanding that we all struggle."
— *Charles F. Glassman* —

generosity is *spoken.*

#97

Speak well of others. There is so much negativity in this world, and much of it is born from speaking negatively. Be a source of positivity in your circle of influence, especially when it comes to speaking about other people.

"Charity, by which God and neighbor are loved, is the most perfect friendship."

— St. Thomas Aquinas —

generosity is *enthralling*.

#98

Become intimately familiar with your talents and abilities. Knowing who you are and what your gifts are is essential to living a life of astounding generosity.

"I believe that in the end it is kindness and generous accommodation that are the catalysts for real change."
— Nelson Mandela —

generosity is *unifying.*

#99

Choose unity. Isolation and separation are destroying us. Generosity chooses togetherness and unity. Seek the path that brings people together. In this unity we will all rediscover the nobility of our humanity.

"I want you to be concerned about your next-door neighbor. Do you know your next-door neighbor?"
— Mother Teresa —

generosity is *simple.*

#100

Give someone an afternoon of carefree time-lessness—time together with no agenda.

"Time cannot be packaged and ribboned and left under trees for Christmas morning. Time can't be given. But it can be shared."

— Cecilia Ahern —

generosity is *wise*.

#101

We have all been wise and we have all been fools. But let us not be fools in this matter, for it is one of life's supreme lessons. Only a fool loves a gift more than the giver of the gift. Life, love, free will, all your fond memories, the dreams that fascinate your heart, everything you've ever had and anything you will have in the future... are all gifts from the Giver of all good things. You owe nothing to anyone other than the Giver of all good things, but to Him you owe everything. Generosity is about recognizing that nothing belongs to us and that everything belongs to Him. It's about embracing our role as stewards of His treasures. It's about listening to His voice and direction, so we know how to enjoy and share all the blessings He has entrusted to us.

PART THREE

insights *and* reflections

———

insights & reflections:

insights & reflections:

insights & reflections:

insights & reflections:

133

insights & reflections:

insights & reflections:

135

insights & reflections:

insights & reflections:

insights & reflections:

insights & reflections:

insights & reflections:

insights & reflections:

insights & reflections:

insights & reflections:

insights & reflections:

insights & reflections:

insights & reflections:

insights & reflections:

insights & reflections:

insights & reflections:

about the author

MATTHEW KELLY is a best-selling author, speaker, thought leader, entrepreneur, consultant, spiritual leader, and innovator.

He has dedicated his life to helping people and organizations become the-best-version-of-themselves. Born in Sydney, Australia, he began speaking and writing in his late teens while he was attending business school. Since that time, 5 million people have attended his seminars and presentations in more than 50 countries.

Today, Kelly is an internationally acclaimed speaker, author, and business consultant. His books have been published in more than 30 languages, have appeared on the *New York Times*, *Wall Street Journal*, and *USA Today* bestseller lists, and have sold more than 50 million copies.

In his early-twenties he developed "the-best-version-of-yourself" concept and has been sharing it in every arena of life for more than twenty-five years. It is quoted by presidents and celebrities, athletes and their coaches, business leaders and innovators, though perhaps it is never more powerfully quoted than when a mother or father asks a child, "Will that help you become the-best-version-of-yourself?"

Kelly's personal interests include golf, music, art, literature, investing, spirituality, and spending time with his wife, Meggie, and their children Walter, Isabel, Harry, Ralph, and Simon.